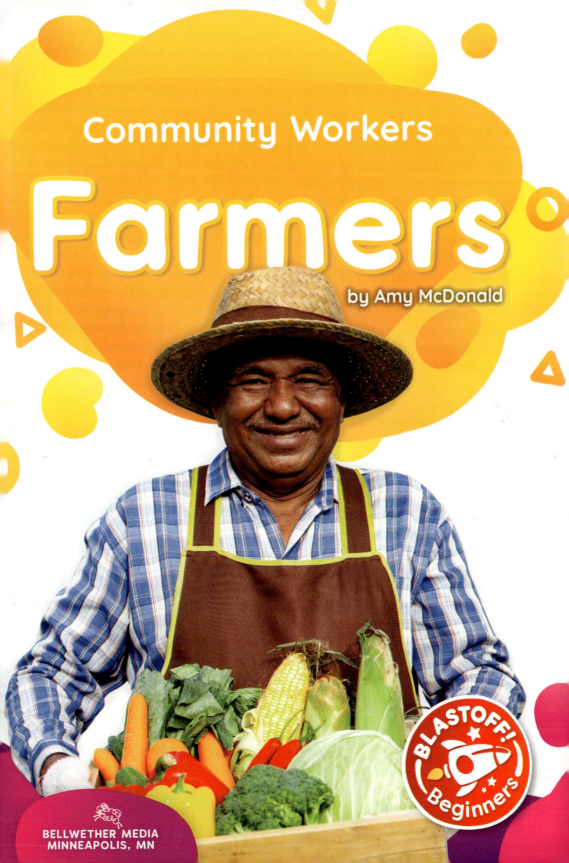

Community Workers
Farmers

by Amy McDonald

BELLWETHER MEDIA • MINNEAPOLIS, MN

Blastoff! Beginners are developed by literacy experts and educators to meet the needs of early readers. These engaging informational texts support young children as they begin reading about their world. Through simple language and high frequency words paired with crisp, colorful photos, Blastoff! Beginners launch young readers into the universe of independent reading.

Sight Words in This Book

a	good	on	to
and	have	some	use
at	help	the	water
big	make	they	what
get	of	this	who

This edition first published in 2025 by Bellwether Media, Inc.

No part of this publication may be reproduced in whole or in part without written permission of the publisher. For information regarding permission, write to Bellwether Media, Inc., Attention: Permissions Department, 6012 Blue Circle Drive, Minnetonka, MN 55343.

Library of Congress Cataloging-in-Publication Data

LC record for Farmers available at: https://lccn.loc.gov/2024038076

Text copyright © 2025 by Bellwether Media, Inc. BLASTOFF! BEGINNERS and associated logos are trademarks and/or registered trademarks of Bellwether Media, Inc.

Editor: Betsy Rathburn   Designer: Laura Sowers

Printed in the United States of America, North Mankato, MN.

Table of Contents

On the Job	4
What Are They?	6
What Do They Do?	10
Why Do We Need Them?	20
Farmer Facts	22
Glossary	23
To Learn More	24
Index	24

On the Job

Who grew this food?
A farmer!

What Are They?

Farmers grow food.

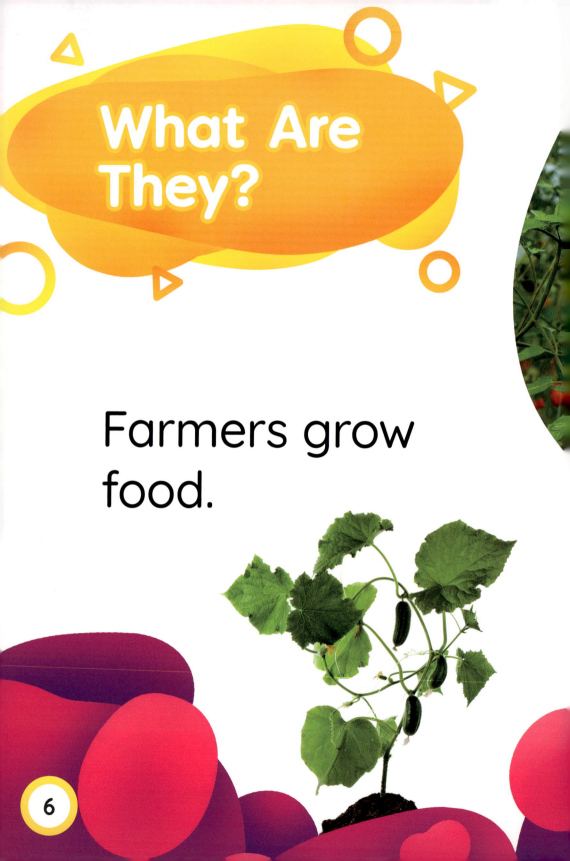

They work on farms. They need a lot of land.

farm

What Do They Do?

Some farmers have animals. Animals make eggs, milk, or meat.

eggs

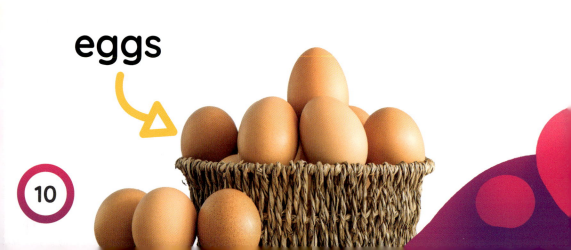

Farmers feed the animals. They clean **pens**.

pens

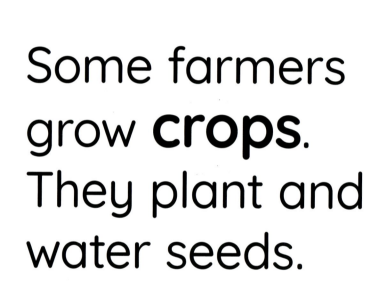

Some farmers grow **crops**. They plant and water seeds.

crop

They **harvest** what grows.
They use big machines.

machines

17

Farmers sell food to stores. Some sell at **markets.**

market

Why Do We Need Them?

Farmers help us get good food. Yum!

Farmer Facts

Tools

seeds

big machines

pens

A Day in the Life

feed animals

grow crops

sell food

22

Glossary

crops
plants that are grown to be sold

harvest
to gather crops

markets
places where people buy and sell goods

pens
homes for farm animals

To Learn More

ON THE WEB

FACTSURFER

Factsurfer.com gives you a safe, fun way to find more information.

1. Go to www.factsurfer.com.
2. Enter "farmers" into the search box and click 🔍.
3. Select your book cover to see a list of related content.

Index

animals, 10, 12
clean, 12
crops, 14
eggs, 10
farms, 8
feed, 12
food, 4, 6, 18, 20
grow, 4, 6, 14, 16
harvest, 16
land, 8
machines, 16, 17
markets, 18, 19
meat, 10
milk, 10
pens, 12
plant, 14
seeds, 14
sell, 18
stores, 18
water, 14
work, 8

The images in this book are reproduced through the courtesy of: PitukTV, front cover; Dushlik, p. 3; Serg64, pp. 4-5 (vegetables); Kostiantyn Voitenko, pp. 4-5; Madlen, p. 6; Tom Wang, pp. 6-7; Nicholas J Klein, p. 8; PeopleImages - Yuri A, pp. 8-9; Marquess789, p. 10; Sirisak_baokaew, pp. 10-11; Marmalade Photos, p. 12; Ground Picture, pp. 12-13; Ms_wittaya, p. 14; SeventyFour, pp. 14-15; jodie777, pp. 16-17; Hispanolistic, pp. 18-19; BearFotos, pp. 20-21; Pawel Gegotek, p. 22 (seeds); Dusan Petkovic, p. 22 (pens); GordanD, p. 22 (big machines); Jenoche, p. 22 (feed animals); Lenin Suntaxi, p. 22 (grow crops); Gorodenkoff, p. 22 (sell food); SoneNS, p. 23 (crops); Jan van Broekhoven, p. 23 (harvest); Tim Childers, p. 23 (markets); Guillermo Spelucin R, p. 23 (pens).